Oracle VM VirtualBox 4.0
on OS X Snow Leopard
Ronald McCarty

This book is also available as an e-book. The picture above is the cover graphic from the e-book version.

Oracle VM VirtualBox 4.0 on OS X Snow Leopard
Copyright (c) 2011

By Ronald W. McCarty, Jr.

About the Author

Ron McCarty is a freelance writer, information technology consultant, and the owner of Your Net Guard LLC, an IT consulting company located in Dallas, Texas.

Ron has written for numerous publications and web sites including Tech Target, CMP, Cisco Press, and New Riders. Topics have included information security, compliancy and controls such as PCI DSS, Linux, and general networking topics.

He completed his bachelor's degree in information systems with the University of Maryland, and his master's degree in management with Capella University. Ron's experience includes 15 years in the technology field and he is a veteran of the first Persian Gulf War.

Ron enjoys suburban life outside Dallas with his wife Claudia, and two children.

Contacting the Author

Ron can be reached at:

email: mccarty@YourNetGuard.com
blog: ron.YourNetGuard.com
twitter: @ronmccarty
web: www.YourNetGuard.com
Publications: http://ron.yournetguard.com/publications.htm

Dedication

This book is dedicated to my daughter, Janice. As a teenager and mid-lifer, she and I don't always see eye-to-eye. Luckily our disagreements are often on things that seem important at the time, but generally are simply laughing points later. Her intelligence, willingness to listen and learn, and bringing calmness and logic to her friends make me very proud. She is currently trying to decide her path into adulthood and career. Whatever path she takes will be challenging, fruitful, and continue to make me a proud father.

Contents

Chapter 1: Introduction to Virtualization

Virtualization has recently become a very hot topic for information technology professionals. Virtualization, along with storage technology, has been one of the major driving forces behind many recent technology projects. Virtualization is also the underlying technology often used in cloud technology--especially in services requiring dynamic allocations of new systems.

Guests and Hosts

At the basic level, virtualized systems are self-contained operating systems that run on top of another operating system. A virtualized system is called a virtual machine (VM) and is considered the "guest." The system installed directly on the hardware is referred to the hypervisor and is considered the "host."

Virtualization was originally created by IBM for mainframes. Virtualization allowed very expensive computing resources to be "carved" into partitions referred to as logical partitions, or LPARs. These LPARs could then execute code independent of each other and appeared as separate systems to the applications.

Current virtualization is similar to the original virtualization created by IBM; however, the reasons for virtualizing far outnumber the reasons for LPARs in the 1960's.

Why Virtualize?

Often software, hardware, and organizations (people) do not play well together; therefore, operating systems need to be installed separately. Prior to virtualization, each install required separate servers. Let's examine some examples from each of these reasons for using virtualization.

Software

An example of software not playing well together is dedicated application servers that are tied to particular versions of a database. The company needs to keep all of the databases current; however, upgrading this particular application's database is not an option until the software vendor has updated their code. This application can be installed on a virtualized system ("virtual machine" or VM) and run on the same hardware as other systems; whereas before the server would have required dedicated hardware.

Hardware

A lot of money can be saved on hardware costs in large companies in the previous example, as servers are stacked on processors that are ever-growing in power. Additionally, legacy servers may need to be upgraded; however the operating system being used may not have appropriate drivers for the hardware. (Often network interface card and storage drivers are issues.) The system can be virtualized though, and the virtualization will handle driver issues for the underlying hardware and allow the legacy operating system to be installed on newer hardware.

Organization

Organization structure and needs often can be met with virtualization. Often organizations within a company have common platform needs (for example, Linux servers), but have different availability, application, and even political wants. For example, the marketing department may be fine with taking a server down every weekend; however, the manufacturing department can only have outages during off shifts every two weeks. Putting these two departments on the same system is less than ideal. Two virtualized systems can be used to meet these needs and can possibly even be placed on a common hardware server, assuming IT can meet the greater of the availability needs on the hardware (i.e., they do not expect to shut down the hardware server to meet marketing's needs, which would then inadvertently hurt manufacturing).

Virtualization for Workstations

We have covered the reasons information technology professionals use virtualization and why they use it.

Virtualization also has many uses on the desktop, and this book covers the use of virtualization on the desktop and on OS X 10.6 Snow Leopard specifically. Virtualization allows other operating systems to run on the computer while leaving the underlying operating system in its native state.

There are numerous reasons for doing this, and some of the most common ones are running applications the native operating system does not support. For example, it is not uncommon for technical consultants who use Macs to run Visio under Windows as a virtual machine. Why do they use Visio and Windows whenever there are numerous Mac drawing programs? Because Visio is often the default drawing format for technology customers.

Another common reason is to test out and review operating systems. For example, there are numerous distributions of Linux, and through virtualization I am able to quickly install and test the latest distributions.

Many times operating systems can be installed without even running an installation. This is accomplished by downloading a virtual box image. This image is basically a copy of the files created after someone has installed an operating system.

Operating systems downloaded and used is this fashion are referred to as appliances, or more specifically software appliances ("soft") to distinguish them from hardware appliances. Numerous appliances are available for VirtualBox from VirtualBoxImages.com (http://virtualboximages.com/).

Oracle also has multiple developer appliances here: http://www.oracle.com/technetwork/community/developer-vms-192663.html.

Software vendors also take advantage of appliances and distribute their software via software appliances. This allows prospects to view the software without being bothered with a software or operating system install.

Virtualization can also be used to run an operating system that you may need for a project. For example, you may need to test the installation process of installing Windows 2008. A virtual machine will allow you to do this easily without having any additional hardware.

Summary

The reasons and uses for virtualization have been covered briefly. There is no better way to appreciate virtualization than to jump right in and try. Luckily, due to Oracle's freely-available VM VirtualBox 4.0, you can easily try and use virtualization on your favorite Mac computer running OS X 10.6. The rest of this book shows you how.

Enjoy!

Chapter 1: Introduction to Virtualization

Chapter 2: Introduction to System Elements

Prior to getting into the actual installation and configuration of VirtualBox, acquiring an understanding of what makes up a virtual machine is necessary. A virtual machine needs all the same elements that a normal computer needs to operate: processor(s), memory, disks, and network interface (NIC) cards.

These elements are borrowed and shared from the real machine. The elements are also shared with other virtual machines running on the system. Although this sharing contains complex algorithms to ensure the best performances, for installation and configuration it is important to understand initially what the elements are and what to consider during installation of a virtual machine.

Processor

The central processing unit (CPU) or processor is the chip responsible for most of the computations necessary to perform operations. Processors in personal computers are typically either Intel or AMD, although there are other offerings from IBM, Arm, and others.

For virtualization, processors that directly support virtualization are ideal. On the Intel platform, Intel supports its Virtualization Technology™ or Intel VT™. AMD supports its virtualization technology through AMD Virtualization (AMD-VT™)

The hypervisor software will then manage assigning CPU cycles to the virtual machines to ensure a virtual machine (guest) doesn't impact the host operating system or other guests on the system.

VirtualBox limits the number of processors that can be used by the machine by setting the number of "cores" assigned to the virtual machine. Cores are individual processors and the terminology is necessary because a processor is often made up of multiple processors that can be individually used.

By allowing a virtual machine to only use a limited number of cores, the hypervisor can be assured cores are available for itself.

Memory

Memory is where the computer keeps data while the data is needed by the user. For example, whenever you are editing a document in a word processor, the document is loaded into memory for you. Memory is very fast compared to hard drives, so its major storage advantage is how quick it can be accessed--quick enough to be considered real time by the user.

The amount of memory in a computer is limited; however at times there is a need to temporarily load more things into memory than your system can hold. To allow this, virtual memory is used. Virtual memory has nothing to do with system virtualization. Virtual memory is created by using a part of the hard drive (swap drive or swap space) as memory temporarily. The operating system can then write to this space as if it is memory. To increase operating system speed, the operating system actually tries to "move" something that isn't currently active from the real memory to the virtual memory. This swapping does take time; however, by moving something inactive, the user's current active program will keep moving at normal speed once the swapping has completed.

Disks

Computers need a storage place to keep our applications and data, and we typically use disks for this. Early personal computers actually used floppy disks, which were 5.25" wide. They were made of a flexible plastic that covered the media. Hard drives, which is the technology we use now, became popular as the amount of processing power increased and as computers became widespread. Although the technology has improved drastically in speed, the basic technology has remained the same--a spindle with magnetic discs.

Virtual machines also require storage for the operating system, applications, and data. However, a virtualized disk is used by the virtual machine. A virtualized disk is actually a file on the hypervisor operating system. Because of the use of a file, the virtual machine can actually be quite easily moved from machine to machine, either via a network or some other storage media such as a DVD or thumb drive.

The file used by VirtualBox to represent the hard drive is referred to as a Virtual Disk Image (VDI) and uses the .vdi extension as identification. The VDI has a standard format and can be used for storing the various operating systems' file system formats, such as ext3 for Linux or NTFS for Windows.

Network Interface Cards

A system connects to the local area network and Internet using its network interface card (NIC). The NIC can be a part of the motherboard, a separate card in the machine, or even connected externally via a USB port. On most new personal computers and all Macs, the NIC card is integrated with the motherboard.

The NIC has a built-in hardware address that uniquely identifies the card worldwide. This hardware address is the Ethernet address and although it is globally unique, it is only used on the local area network. An Internet address, or Internet Protocol (IP) address is assigned to the Ethernet address. You can either manually configure the IP, or it can be provisioned to receive its address dynamically from your router or Internet service provider's router.

The Internet Protocol requires that IP addresses be globally unique; unfortunately, there are not enough IP addresses available with the current version of the protocol. Therefore, we use a technique called network address translation (NAT) in which your Internet provider gives you a single globally unique address. This address is then used to translate to your internal IP addressees. This concept is also used by virtual machines, as we'll see shortly.

Most likely, you'll want to use your virtual machines on your network and Internet as well. To do so, you'll need to have the virtual machine on your local area network. VirtualBox (and most virtualization systems) supports two modes of operating on your network: NAT and bridged.

In NAT mode, your virtual machine is not assigned Ethernet or IP addresses. Rather, it uses the host's address to send out traffic. The hypervisor tracks the traffic and maintains a NAT table to accept responses back to the traffic. In this mode, the virtual machine is useful for client (user) operations, but isn't useful as a server.

In bridge mode, the virtual machine has an Ethernet address and IP address. The IP address assignment can be either manually configured (within the virtual machine) or it can be dynamically configured from your router or Internet service provider. Since the machine is on the network, this mode is ideal whenever you wish to run server software (such as a mail server) on the virtual machine. (Note: The IP address is still on your local area network, so most likely, you will have to use NAT at your Internet gateway to make the system globally reachable for server software such as mail servers.)

Summary

This chapter provided a brief overview of the elements that make a computer system useful and how the elements are supported in a virtual machine. Now that the basics are covered, the next chapter will cover VirtualBox installation.

Chapter 3: Installation of Oracle VM VirtualBox 4.0

In order to install VirtualBox on a system, there are some prerequisites that must be met. Since you are reading how to install VirtualBox 4.0 on Snow Leopard, your computer most likely meets the prerequisites. VirtualBox 4.0 will also run on Leopard (version 10.5 of OS X). An Intel-based Mac is required.

The software install requires about 200 MB of free space. Each guest operating system will require between 2 GB and 20 GB typically. For our example we use Cent OS 5.5, and an 8 GB virtual disk image.

Download

VirtualBox is freely available from a link on this page: http://www.oracle.com/us/technologies/virtualization/oraclevm/061976.html. It is also available at the open source site at http://www.virtualbox.org. The Oracle license currently allows for individual use and single user business license use.

Once you download VirtualBox, you'll need to open the disk image (.dmg file) from your Downloads folder by double clicking it. Once you double click it, you'll see the disk image contents as shown in the following figure.

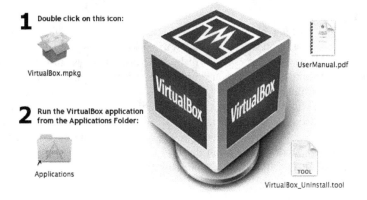

Install

Start the installation by double clicking the VirtualBox.mpkg icon. The installation will start off by warning you that you should not run any software that you do not trust its source as shown here:

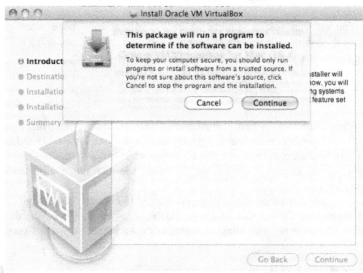

After clicking on the Continue button from the install warning, the installer will ask you where to install VirtualBox. Unless you have more than one disk drive the only option will be your operating system drive (usually named Macintosh HD). If you do have more than one drive, then you may install the application where you wish. The installer is only picking the application's install location--you will be able to install virtual machines to other disk drives on the computer.

Once you select the location, you'll be provided the option to select a custom installation as shown in the next figure. For this installation, do not customize the install, and simply click Install.

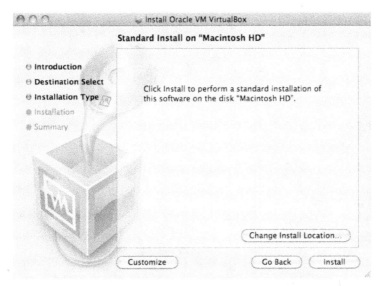

The install process will take a few minutes to install its binaries and supporting files. It will install the binaries in the Applications folder, and finish with this screen:

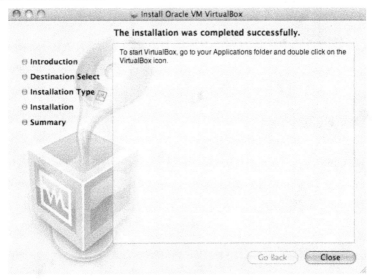

Finish

VirtualBox is now ready to be used. Double click on its icon in the Application folder and keep reading!

Chapter 4: Creation of a Virtual Machine

Now that VirtualBox has been installed, we can jump right into creating a virtual machine. Whenever creating a virtual machine, you need to know the operating system you will be installing, and in this example we will use CentOS 5.5.

New Machine

If the VirtualBox Manager isn't still running, start it back up and you should see the welcome screen:

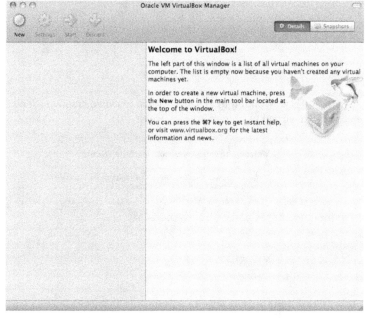

In the upper left corner of the screen, you'll see a new button:

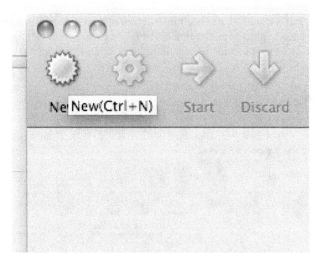

Click on the new button to start the virtual machine creation. You'll be greeted with the virtual machine wizard process:

Naming the Virtual Machine

Click on the Continue button. You'll then be asked to tell VirtualBox the name of the virtual machine as well as the OS type and version. This part of the wizard will actually try to guess the operating system type based upon what you type. In the next two examples, you can see where it guesses Windows when I typed Wind, and Linux when I typed CentOS.

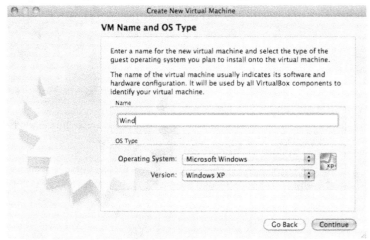

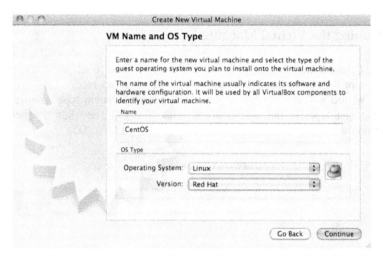

Type in the name you would like to call the virtual machine. This is the name of the directory that the virtual machine will create within your home directory in the VirtualBox VMs subdirectory.

For the Operating System choose Linux, and for the version use Red Hat or Red Hat 64-bit if you downloaded the 64-bit version of CentOS.

Memory

Once you've entered the name, OS, and OS version, click on Continue. The wizard will now ask you for the amount of memory to assign to the system:

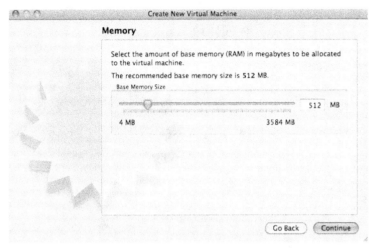

The wizard's memory recommendation should be followed as a minimum. The color bar across the bottom of the slider shows you the impact to the system. Whenever you give a virtual machine enough memory so that it is in the orange or red, it will most likely impact system performance, as it is using a large majority of the system's real memory.

Use 512-MB for the time being--you can always easily change it later. Click on Continue, and the system will then ask how the virtual disk should be set up. The wizard wants to know if you wish to boot from the hard disk and whether to create a new or use an existing:

Generally you will always want to boot from the disk and create a new one. Select the options to do so, and then click Continue.

New Virtual Disk Wizard

Once you click Continue, the wizard will kick off the Create New Virtual Disk Wizard:

Click Continue to let the disk wizard continue. The wizard will then prompt you to decide the type of disk you wish to create: dynamic or fixed-size. The dynamic disk size is the fastest to create as it will create a small file and expand the file when needed; however, it can be slower over time as the growing of the file is a bit slower than when the file already exists. The fixed-size file will take longer to create; however, it will be faster over the long run as expanding the file will not use additional time. I generally use the dynamic whenever I run virtual machines on workstations, and static whenever I'm running virtual machines on servers. (Having a virtual machine lock up on a server farm because it doesn't have disk space available because another machine or application used it causes havoc.)

For this book, I chose the dynamic option:

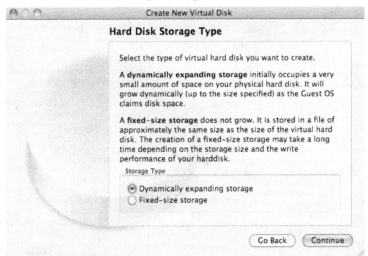

After choosing the type of virtual disk, you are now prompted to identify the name of the disk and its size. By default the wizard will use the name of the virtual machine, which is generally a good choice. The size of the disk is actually determined by the size of the operating system plus the size needed for application installs. For this install we are only going to use the system software, so I used 8 GB. Most versions of Linux need between 4- and 8-GB space for the OS with some growth room.

The following figure shows the name and size of the virtual disk selection:

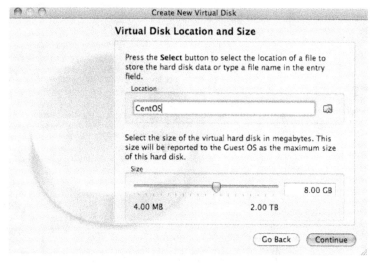

After choosing the name of the virtual disk and its size and pressing Continue, the wizard will give you a summary of the new disk and give you one last chance to correct issues by clicking Go Back. Assuming everything is correct, press Done.

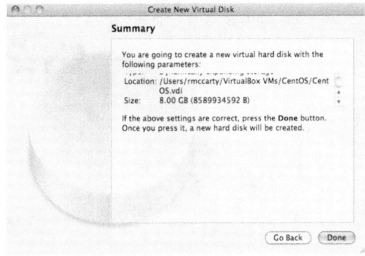

The completion of the Virtual Disk Wizard completes the New Virtual Machine Wizard as well, so VirtualBox will report the machine creation:

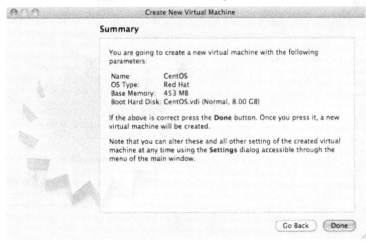

Once you click Done, the wizard will return control to the VirtualBox Manager:

Chapter 5: Installation of CentOS 5.5 on VirtualBox

CentOS 5.5 was chosen for the purpose of this book for several reasons:

- CentOS is freely available on the web, and version 5.5 is the most current version.
- CentOS is based upon Red Hat 5.5 and Red Hat is one of the most popular server distributions.
- Mac users tend to be very happy with their desktop, so they tend to be more interested in looking at and using server operating systems as virtual machines.

Download

CentOS can be downloaded from http://www.centos.org/. The easiest method of install is to use the DVD iso, as you will not need to interact with the install to change disks as you would have to with CDs.

The DVD iso image is approximately 4 GB, so give yourself plenty of time for the download. Some of the mirror sites for CentOS do not include the DVD version, so you will need to either use a different mirror site or download the iso using a torrent client.

CentOS 5.5 comes in two versions: 32-bit and 64-bit. The 32-bit version can be found in the i386 directory on the mirror sites, and the 64-bit version will be in the x86_64 directory.

Once you've downloaded the version you want, go back to the VirtualBox Manager starting screen:

Starting the First Run Wizard

Highlight the CentOS install and press the green arrow start button. This will start the First Run Wizard as shown below. Click on the Continue button...

You can install an operating system from the Mac's built in DVD drive; however there is no need to burn a CentOS install DVD. It can be installed directly from the iso download by clicking on the yellow folder directory and then finding the directory (Downloads, unless you saved it to somewhere else).

The following two screens show this in action:

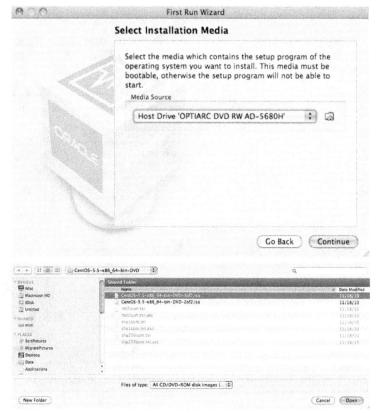

Once you've chosen the iso image, it will show the selection in the Select Installation media screen, as well as giving you a summary of your selection:

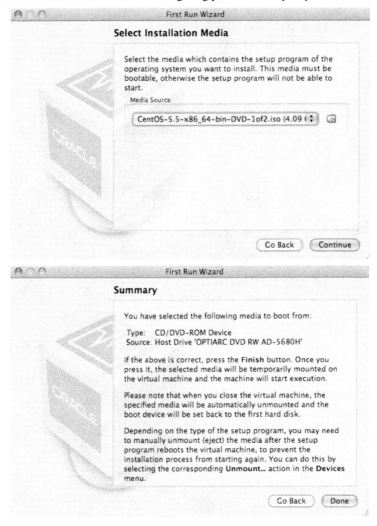

Starting the CentOS 5.5 Install

Select Done and the machine will start to boot up:

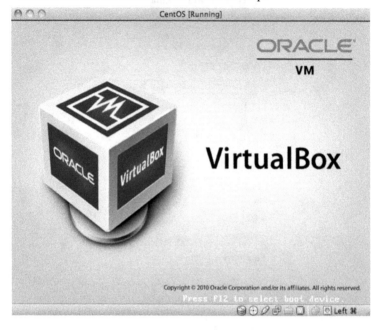

And then show the CentOS boot loader:

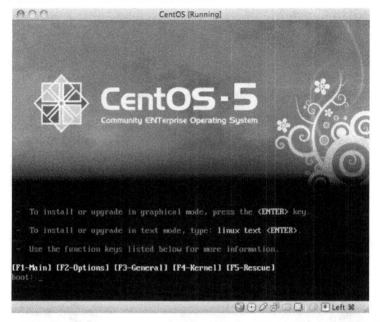

At which time you can press return to start, or it will start automatically for you if wait.

CentOS Check Media

The first step of the CentOS install process is to check the media. Even though the media is actually an ISO image, I generally run the check on the first install of the operating system install to ensure the download was good. You can either perform the media check or skip it as shown here:

CentOS GUI Startup and Language

After the media check, CentOS will start up its GUI screen:

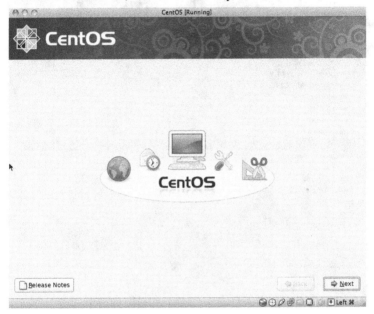

At which time you can click Next, and receive the prompt for the language CentOS should use:

Partitioning Warning

After selecting the language, you'll be prompted for the keyboard layout, and then the installer will warn that it cannot read the partition table on the disk drive. This is normal for all new installs (not just virtual machines) on new disks.

Let the installer initialize the drives by selecting Yes to the question "Would you like to initialize this drive, erasing ALL Data?"

The installer will then walk through the partitioning of the hard drive as shown here:

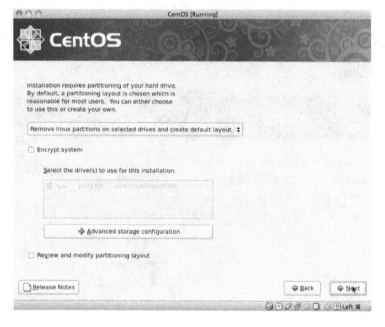

Click on Next and the installer will warn you that it will be erasing data on the drive:

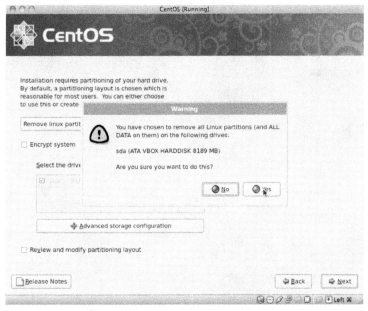

Click Yes on the warning, and the installer will partition the drives, and then prompt you for the network information as shown below.

Allow the system to use DHCP unless you manage IP addresses on your network and wish to manually assign one.

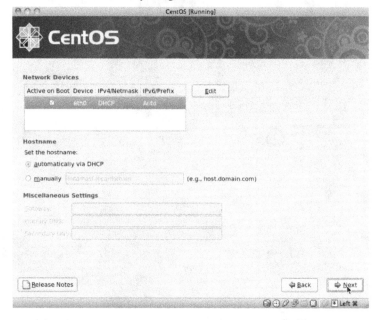

CentOS 5.5 Time Zone and Type of Install

For the next three steps, you'll be prompted for the time zone of the server, the root password, and the type of install. I've included examples here, but assign the fields according to how you would like them.

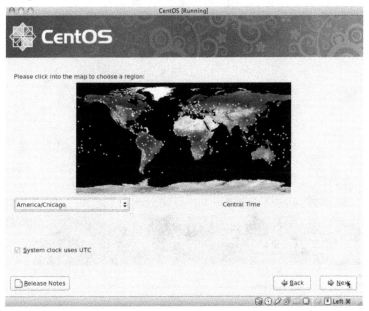

Wrap Up CentOS 5.5 Install

The CentOS installer will then prompt you to continue by clicking Next, at which time it will start copying its packages to the virtual disk drive. Finally it will report it is complete, and ask you to click to reboot. The next three screen shots show this process:

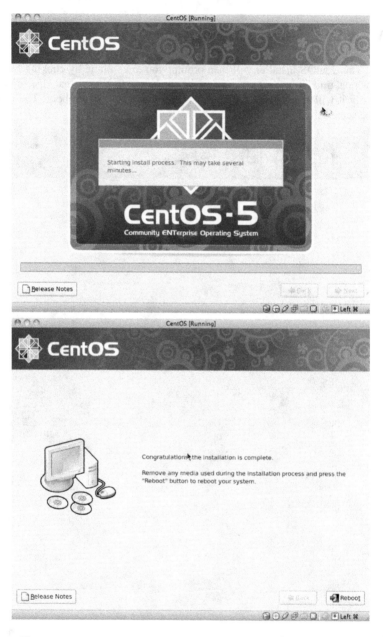

Once the system completes a reboot, you'll receive the CentOS welcome screen:

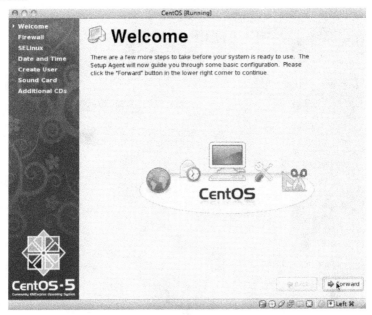

The installer will continue with the firewall configuration.

For the initial install, you will most likely just need the firewall to allow secure shell (ssh) as shown with the default setting:

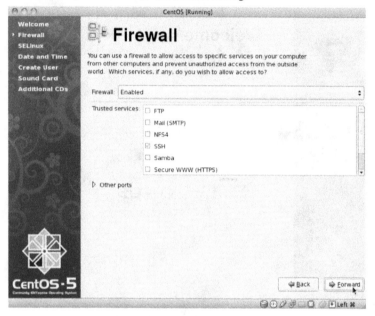

After setting the firewall to allow ssh, the installer will ask you to set the date and time, create your user account, and test the sound card:

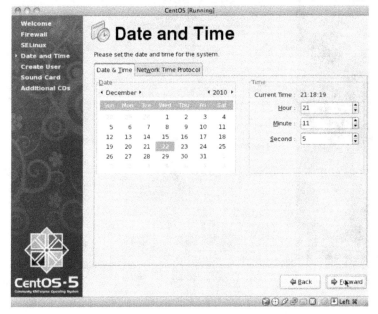

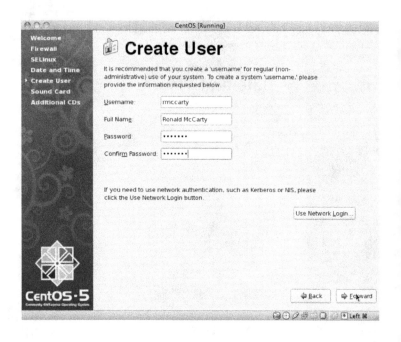

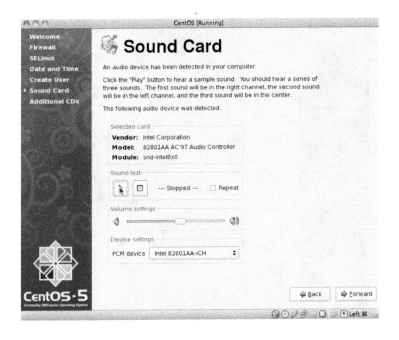

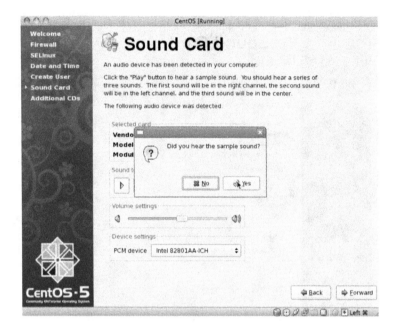

The installer will then ask if you have any additional software to install, which is not required for a standard install, so simply click on Finish:

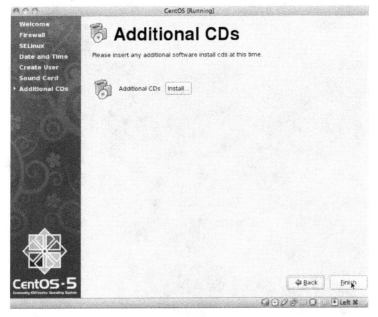

CentOS Login

The install is now complete, and you can log in and see your desktop in CentOS 5.5.

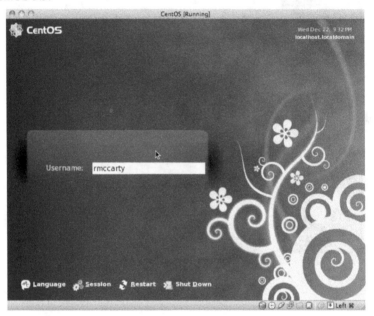

Chapter 5: Installation of CentOS 5.5 on VirtualBox

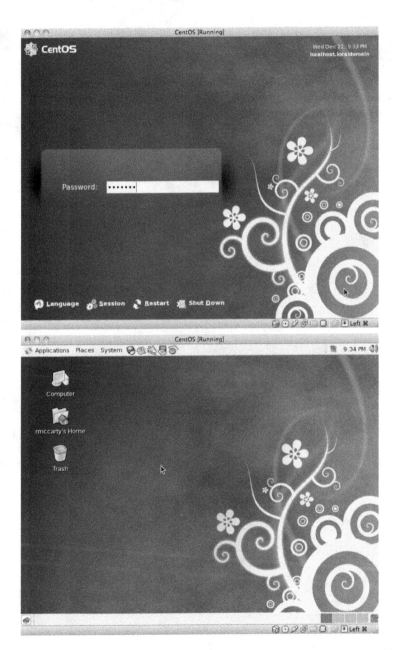

Complete

That wraps it up! I hope this book has been useful, concise, and just what you were looking for. I welcome your comments, critique, and feedback. You can reach me at: mccarty@YourNetGuard.com.